It's My Body

Hair

Lola M. Schaefer

Heinemann Library
Chicago, Illinois

Designed by Sue Emerson, Heinemann Library; Page layout by Que-Net Media
Printed and bound in the China
Photo research by Jennifer Gillis

12 11 10 09
10 9 8 7 6 5

Library of Congress Cataloging-in-Publication Data
Schaefer, Lola M., 1950-
  Hair / Lola M. Schaefer.
       v. cm. – (It's my body)
Includes index.
Contents: What is your hair? – Where does your hair grow? – What does your hair look like? – What does your hair feel like? – How does your hair grow? – What happens to your hair? – How does hair help you? – How do eyebrows help you? – How do eyelashes help you? – Quiz – Picture glossary.
  ISBN 1-4034-0893-9 (HC), 1-4034-3480-8 (Pbk.)
  ISBN 978-1-4034-0893-8 (HC), 978-1-4034-3480-7 (Pbk.)
  1. Hair–Juvenile literature. [1. Hair. 2. Human anatomy.] I. Title. II. Series.
  QM488 .S335 2003
  612.7'99–dc21

2002014737

Acknowledgments
The author and publishers are grateful to the following for permission to reproduce copyright material:
p. 4 Larry Williams/Corbis; p. 5 Ariel Skelley/Corbis; p. 6 Janet Moran/Heinemann Library; pp. 7, 10, 11, 18, 20, 21, 22, 23, 24 Brian Warling/Heinemann Library; p. 8 David Young-Wolff/PhotoEdit; p. 9 Rold Bruderer/Corbis; p. 13 Custom Medical Stock Photo; pp. 14, 15 Greg Williams/Heinemann Library; p. 16 Chris Arend/Alaska Stock Images/PictureQuest; p. 17, 19 Robert Lifson/Heinemann Library; back cover Brian Warling/Heinemann Library

Cover photograph by Brian Warling/Heinemann Library

Every effort has been made to contact copyright holders of any material reproduced in this book. Any omissions will be rectified in subsequent printings if notice is given to the publisher.

Special thanks to our advisory panel for their help in the preparation of this book:
Alice Bethke, Library Consultant
Palo Alto, CA

Eileen Day, Preschool Teacher
Chicago, IL

Kathleen Gilbert,
Second Grade Teacher
Round Rock, TX

Sandra Gilbert,
Library Media Specialist
Fiest Elementary School
Houston, TX

Jan Gobeille,
Kindergarten Teacher
Garfield Elementary
Oakland, CA

Angela Leeper,
Educational Consultant
North Carolina Department
of Public Instruction
Wake Forest, NC

Some words are shown in bold, **like this.**
You can find them in the picture glossary on page 23.

Contents

What Is Your Hair?

Your hair is part of your body.

Your body is made up of
many parts.

Each part of your body does a job.

Your hair helps keep you warm.

Where Does Hair Grow?

Hair grows on people's heads.

It grows on arms, legs, hands, and feet, too.

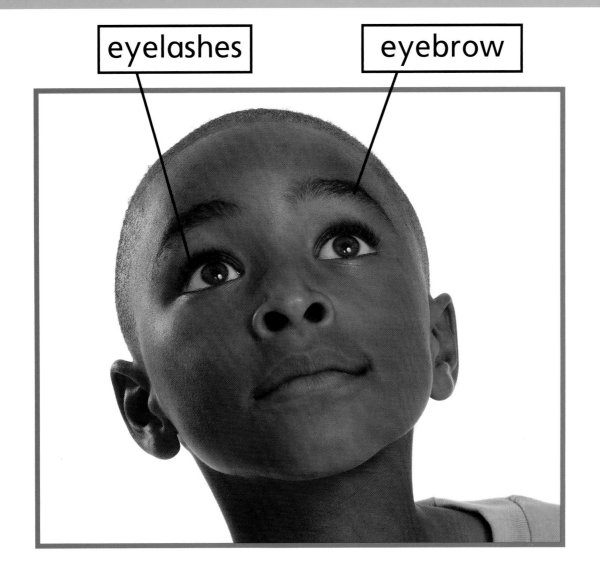

eyelashes

eyebrow

Hair grows on your face.

Eyelashes and **eyebrows** are made of hair.

What Does Your Hair Look Like?

Hair can be black, brown, yellow, or red.

Some hair is gray or white.

Hair can be curly or straight.

It can be short or long.

What Does Your Hair Feel Like?

Some hair feels smooth and soft.

Other hair feels thick and wavy.

Hair can feel fuzzy.

It can feel prickly.

How Does Your Hair Grow?

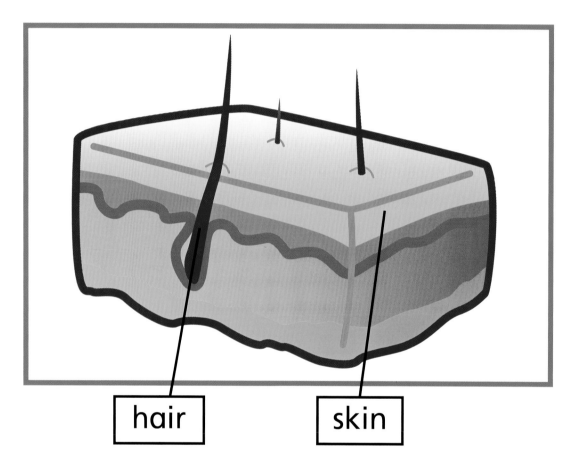

hair

skin

Hair starts under the skin.

It looks like a thin thread.

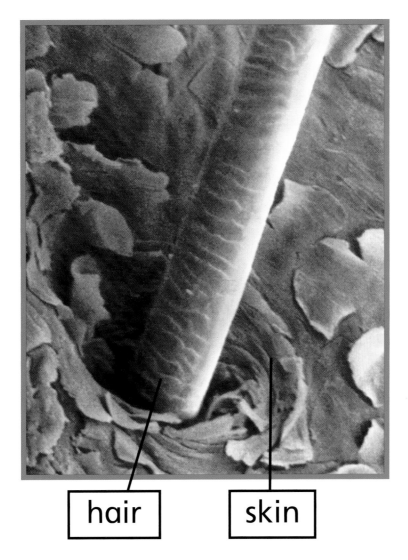

hair   skin

Hair comes out of the skin.

This picture makes a little hair look big.

What Happens to Your Hair?

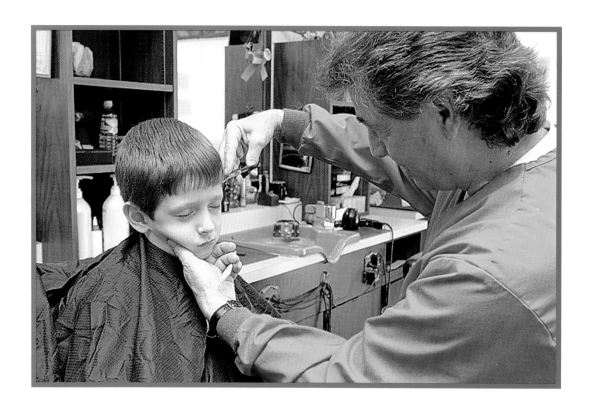

Your hair grows and grows.

If you didn't cut it, it would get very long.

Hair falls out when it stops growing.

New hair grows to take its place.

How Does Hair Help You?

Some hair keeps parts of your body safe.

Hair can keep snow off people's faces.

Hair helps keep your head safe
from the sun.

How Do Eyebrows Help You?

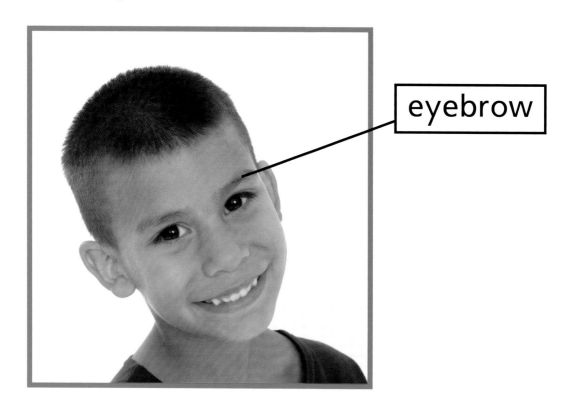

eyebrow

Your **eyebrows** help keep your eyes safe.

Eyebrows keep things out of your eyes.

Eyebrows can keep sweat out of your eyes.

They can keep dirt out of your eyes, too.

How Do Eyelashes Help You?

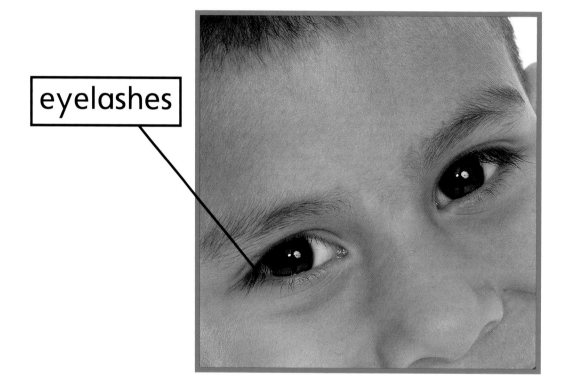

eyelashes

Eyelashes help keep your eyes safe.

You have many eyelashes all around your eyes.

Eyelashes clean the air when you blink.

They sweep the dust away from your eyes.

Quiz

Can you guess what these are?

Look for the answers on page 24.

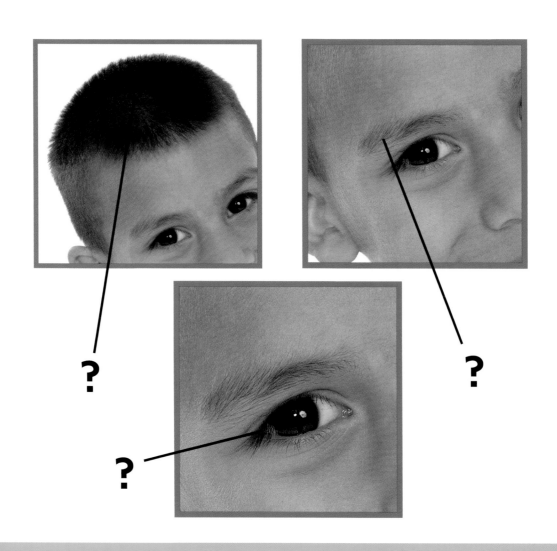

Picture Glossary

eyebrows
pages 7, 18, 19

eyelashes
pages 7, 20, 21

Note to Parents and Teachers

Reading for information is an important part of a child's literacy development. Learning begins with a question about something. Help children think of themselves as investigators and researchers by encouraging their questions about the world around them. Each chapter in this book begins with a question. Read the question together. Look at the pictures. Talk about what you think the answer might be. Then read the text to find out if your predictions were correct. Think of other questions you could ask about the topic, and discuss where you might find the answers. Assist children in using the picture glossary and the index to practice new vocabulary and research skills.

Index

Answers to quiz on page 22

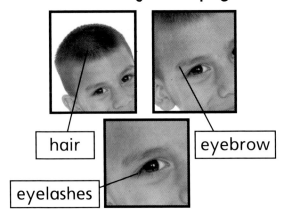

hair

eyebrow

eyelashes